SUPER

DYNAMIC KICKS

BY CHONG LEE

- •AUTHOR OF DYNAMIC KICKS
- •AUTHOR OF ADVANCED EXPLOSIVE KICKS

SUPER DYNAMIC KICKS

BY CHONG LEE
- •AUTHOR OF DYNAMIC KICKS
- •AUTHOR OF ADVANCED EXPLOSIVE KICKS

Graphic Design by Marcia Mack

WARNING

OHARA 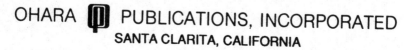 PUBLICATIONS, INCORPORATED
SANTA CLARITA, CALIFORNIA

Dedication

To my mother and father,
and to my wife, Cindy

Acknowledgement

To my best students and fellow instructors,
Danny Gibson and Nick King

About the Author

Chong Lee—a man in motion. His reputation in the martial arts is well-established: Born in Korea, he earned his first-degree black belt in tae kwon do at the age of seven. At 11, he took up Thai kickboxing, and it wasn't until after he had broken his forearm, his jaw (twice), and several toes, that he perfected his technique in the art.

When he came to the United States, he had to modify his full-contact training to conform to the American form of no-contact karate. Eventually, he developed his own unique style—a combination of forms and full-contact fighting. It was a style which earned him the Forms Grand Championship at the 1974 Long Beach Internationals.

So it has been firmly established that when Chong Lee does something, he puts everything he has into it. And now that includes the real estate business. He recently started his own real estate investment office now that his six-year old karate studio has flourished; no doubt due to his energetic efforts.

"Before, my life was karate one hundred percent," he once

said. "Now I've expanded, and I have more respect for individuals both in and out of the martial arts.

"Still, when I'm teaching I'm very strict. It's 'do this' and 'do that.' But after class I don't even think about it."

What he does think about, besides karate and real estate, are his hobbies which include running and flying. In fact, he is planning to earn a pilot's license in the near future. In the meantime, he and his wife, Cindy, live very comfortably reaping the benefits from the well-channeled efforts of this driven businessman and athlete.

—Ohara Publications

Preface

This is not a book for beginners.

It is for the student who has already read Chong Lee's other two books: *Dynamic Kicks* and *Advanced Explosive Kicks.* It contains the most advanced techniques developed to help the student learn what is perhaps the most difficult aspect of the martial arts.

Part one, "Simple Kicks," is a warm-up for the student. It contains three basic maneuvers which the student will be able to build upon in later chapters.

Part two, "Kick and Punch Combination," combines the beauty and dynamics of the kick with the power of the punch/counterpunch combination.

Part three, "Running Jumping Kick," contains eight combination kicks which utilize all of the student's kicking abilities.

Part four, "Air-Kick Combinations," displays perhaps the most graceful, yet most effective, kicking techniques in the martial arts.

Daily practice of these skills is certain to sharpen a student's abilities to the fullest. As Chong Lee once said, "All men have two legs that function in certain ways, and there exist standard principles for making these legs work most efficiently and most powerfully." *Super Dynamic Kicks III* puts all those principles together.

Contents

Techniques Basic To All Kicks

More than anything, the secret to effective kicking is the successful combination of excellent timing, rhythm and speed. Those three aspects in freefighting make it possible for a student to deliver 100 percent of his potential force. In fact, if a fighter exploits an opponent's reaction time or his momentum, he should be able to strike with 200 percent or even 300 percent of his ordinary force.

If the kick is faster than the hand, which it should be after constant training, it should also be capable of delivering five times as much power as the hand. To understand that point, always keep this equation in mind:

$$Weight \times Speed = Power$$

In other words, the lighter your body weight, the more speed you will be required to develop in your kick in order to deliver the same power generated by a slower, but heavier, fighter. The velocity of your kicks will ultimately depend on the elasticity of your body, the control of your breath, the accuracy of your aim, and the intensity of your concentration.

Dynamic kicking is not just executed with the feet. Your legs, waist, ankles, toes and hips are also important. And the more you are able to incorporate and coordinate these elements into your kicks, the more power you will have. For example, although the flexibility of your ankle is a very important factor in determining your kicking ability, the actual velocity of the kick is, perhaps more than anything else, determined by the power expended in the snap of the

ankle.

As you practice the techniques outlined in this book, keep the following five points in mind:

Use Full Power Only at Full Extension—

Remember, tension not only hinders your speed, but it exhausts your strength very early. Many beginners tend to use full strength throughout the entire kick. This is wasteful and unnecessary, because although kicks should always be delivered at top speed, the entire leg should remain relaxed until the moment of full extension or just before contact. Then, full extension and muscle power should be concentrated in a powerful burst.

Raise the Kicking Leg and Knee Up High—

In order to execute a variety of kicks in one smooth motion, the knee should be raised as high as possible prior to flexing. There are three main reasons for this:

1. The straighter the plane on which it travels, the more forceful the kick will be. In other words, the more the trajectory of your kick moves in a straight horizontal line parallel to the floor, the more potent it will be. Just imagine your foot as an arrow being delivered from your own waist, level to the waist of your opponent.

2. Kicking from such a high position allows your opponent less time to react. With the kick cocked high, it can shoot out to a wider variety of targets. Then it becomes more difficult for your opponent to guess where you intend to strike him.

Continued

3. A kick thrown from a high position is harder to block. If your kick is driven up from the ground directly to the target, it can be stopped when your opponent lowers his forearm. But with your knee cocked high in the air, it will be much more difficult for your opponent to decide how he will block your kick, especially if he doesn't know where you intend to kick him.

The wise fighter never begins with his kicking foot swept back toward the knee of his supporting leg. With his knee drawn back, the kicker cannot react as swiftly to his opponent. For example, picture yourself being faced with an opponent's oncoming head punch. You spot an opening to his rib cage, and you are hoping to deliver a side kick before his punch lands. But if you cock your knee before you can raise it again to execute the kick, your opponent's punch will connect. Instead, you should have raised the knee of your kicking leg and shot your kick off from there. Then, even if your kick was too slow to land effectively, it would have acted as a block, halting your opponent's advance, causing his punch to be ineffective.

Maintain A Straight Line Through the Body While Kicking—

Here the object is to make certain you invest more than just the muscular energy of your legs into your kicks. If your hips and whole body are thrust forward into the kick, you can develop tremendous power.

For example, imagine that you are delivering a side kick to a brick wall. Your hip and extended leg are in line, but your body is not. The force of the kick is directed back toward you. And because your trunk and leg are functioning as separate units at this point, the kick will recoil off the brick wall, and the shock of the recoil will be absorbed by your hip joint. Since your trunk and leg are not aligned, your upper body will continue forward as the shock of your kick comes back at your hip joint. The power of such a kick is scattered and misdirected.

If, on the other hand, the entire body, hip and leg are held on the same line, the force of the blow will either break through the wall or repel you backwards. There will be no force to obstruct the full delivery of power. All your weight will be behind it.

Keep Sudden Changes in Movement and Rhythm to a Minimum—

Before and during initiation of any kicking technique, the fighter's body should not undergo major changes in movement that will help his opponent figure out where and when the next attack will arrive. If you are moving, continue to do so until the last instant. If you are still, remain that way until the last instant. Only the leg should move at the start of the kick.

Use Eye Feints and Peripheral Vision—

The clever fighter soon becomes adept at watching his opponent's eyes for telltale signs of where the opponent will launch his attack, while learning tricks of his own to disguise his own intentions. Also, learning to make use of his peripheral vision gives a fighter a wider range of awareness and enables him to spot possible openings for attack.

Striking Areas

As far as kicking is concerned, the martial artist may choose to kick with any of nine different surfaces. Blows delivered with the heel are intended to land either on the bottom or back of the heel. In either case, curl your toes and instep up toward your knee. To strike with the ball of the foot, point with your instep while pulling back with your toes. To hit with the arch of the foot (the area between the heel and ball), you may either point your foot slightly as you would do in executing sweeps, for example, or the foot may be angled in toward the knee as inside kicks and stomps. Kicks thrown with the outside edge of the foot are executed with the the arch curved inward toward your knee in order to insure that the outside area of the foot makes primary contact.

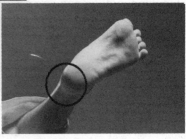

HEEL

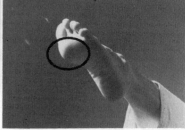

BALL OF THE FOOT

INSIDE OF THE ARCH

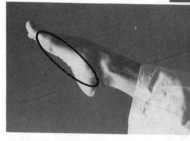

OUTSIDE CRESCENT-SHAPED AREA

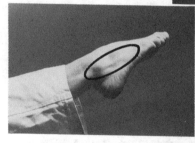

TOP OF THE INSTEP

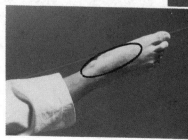

Continued

EXTREME OUTSIDE
EDGE OF THE FOOT

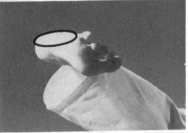

KNEE

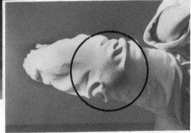

BOTTOM OF THE FOOT

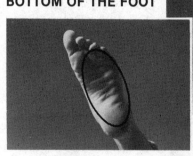

SHIN

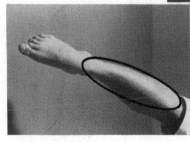

Stretching
Exercises

Knee Bends

Put your feet together (1) and straighten your legs. Begin your squat (2) still holding your hands over your knees (3). Then straighten your legs (4) while continuing to bend forward from the waist, and (5-7) force your knees to revolve in a counterclockwise direction so that you begin two connected motions—a motion involving squatting and standing, and a second revolving movement centered in the knees. Now (8) return to the first position and continue, this time, revolving in a clockwise motion.

Knee Circles

Assuming the same position (1) as for the knee-bend exercise, place the palms of your hands (2) on your knees, keeping your body (3) as still as possible. Then (4) rotate your knees in counterclockwise and (5) clockwise circular motions ten times.

Jump Split

Put your feet together (1), extending your arms slightly and bending at the knees. As your arms extend fully out and backward (2), all your weight should be shifted to the balls of your feet. Then (3) propel yourself upward, kicking your legs out straight, touching your fingertips to your toes.

Isometric Exercises

Elevate your leg to a bar (1) placed about shoulder-height. Then press the heel of your foot against the bar (2-3) as hard as you can for ten seconds and tighten the muscles thoroughout your leg. If no bar is available (4) use a partner to assist you as shown. Then repeat the procedure with your other leg.

Alternate Sitting Knee-Stretch

Sit on the floor (1) with legs extending straight in front of you and feet together. Holding on to your right foot and bending at the knee (2), bring your foot toward your abdomen and (3) place it across your fully extended left thigh as close to the hip joint as possible. Then, bending from the waist, reach out and touch the toes of your left leg. Having returned your right leg to the fully extended position (4) bend forward again touching both toes, and repeat the exercise with the opposite leg.

Reverse Sitting Hip-Stretch

Having settled slowly and gradually into a splits position (1) turn from the hips and bend forward until you can touch your forehead to the floor. Then (2) turn around and repeat exercise from the other side.

Squatting Stretch

Extend your right leg forward with your knee locked (1), bend at the left knee, squat down and fold your hands in front of your waist. Twist and bend forward at the hips. Then lift up from the waist (2), and using the muscles in both legs, raise yourself into a position (3) from which you can shift to the other side. Bend again at the waist (4) and lower your face as far as possible toward the floor. The exercise should be done in one continuous rocking motion, shifting from side to side, until your back and leg muscles are fully relaxed.

Double Straight-Leg Splits Stretch

Having settled slowly and gradually into a splits position (1), lean forward until you can stretch your arms out and reach your toes. While still holding your toes (2), bend forward from your hips until (3) your chin is touching the ground. Repeat this until the muscles in your back and legs are relaxed.

Down-Back Up-Back

Reach down to the floor in front of you (1) by bending at the waist. Keep your knees locked and tighten the hamstring muscles. Come up slightly (2) then touch the floor between and in back of your legs. Come up (3), put your hands on your waist, and (4) arch your back.

Sitting Hamstring-Stretch

Assume the position in (1). Then (2) place your left hand around your left foot. Extend your left leg (3), reaching across and gripping your left kneecap with your right hand. Then (4) stretch the leg straight out and up, while holding onto your knee. Finally (5) retract it.

Squat Kicks

Begin (1) in a squatting position with your knees forming a right angle to the floor and your hands positioned behind your head. Raise up (2) and extend your right leg upward at a 45-degree angle from the rest of your body. Then drop to the ground again (3) assuming the ready position. Repeat the process again (4) this time extending your left leg upward.

2

3

2

3

4

3

4

5

2

3

4

Back Bends

Begin (1) on your back with your knees bent and your hands turned palms down. Then (2&3) push off and at full extension (4) your arms should be completely straight, and your back should be tightly arched. Release tension slowly (5) and descend.

Frog Jump

Begin (1) in a squatting position with your knees forming a right angle to the floor, and your hands positioned behind your head. Simply jump into the air (2) keeping your knees bent and your hands behind your head. As you land, try not to let your knees bend completely; rather, keep them at a right angle.

Double Bent-Leg Sitting Stretch

Sit on the floor (1) spread both legs, and press the soles of your feet together. Then (2) lower your knees as far as possible, and while keeping your back straight, lower your forehead until you can touch your feet. Hold this position (3) for about a minute.

Variation to the Double Bent-Leg Sitting Stretch

Perform the same exercise as above, with someone behind you pressing down on your shoulders to make sure your back muscles are being stretched as much as possible.

3

4

5

2

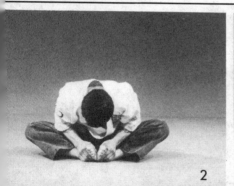
2

3

3

4

5

Simple Kicks

What follows are the three most basic kicks in the martial arts. Once the student has mastered these, he may then continue with the rest of the book, building on them with the various techniques outlined in chapters two, three and four.

It should be pointed out that, although these kicks are simple, they are still very important. It is for that reason that they must be practiced constantly and seriously. Without them, the student will not be able to effectively execute all the variations detailed in this book.

Perform them slowly at first, until you make sure you are doing everything right. Also, in order to develop the muscular strength for advancement, practice holding the kicks at full extension for counts of 10, 20 and 30.

Step Up—Front Kick

Start with your right foot back (1) putting most of your weight on your right leg. Then (2) shift your weight to your left leg, bringing your right leg forward (3) as you reach out with your left hand. Draw your left foot up and forward (4&5) in an arching motion so that your left knee seems to rush toward the left side of your chest. At full extension (6) your left calf muscles and the left side of your stomach should be completely tense, and you should be leaning back slightly, keeping your supporting leg tense to provide you with more hip power. As you release tension (7) retract your left leg and (8) bring your upper body up. Then (9) drop your left leg forward and assume the original stance.

Step Up—Roundhouse Kick

Begin (1) with your right foot in front. Then (2) bring your left foot forward, shifting your weight to your left leg. Begin the kick (3&4) by bringing your right foot up and forward in an arch. Drop your right elbow back as your right hand whips across. At full extension (5), the right side of your back should be tightly arched and your right leg should be completely tense. At this point, you should be looking over your shoulder at your target. Release tension (6) and bring your right leg back with your eyes still on your target. Then (7&8) drop your right leg and assume the original position.

2

4

5

7

8

Step Up—Side Kick

Begin with your right foot forward (1) and most of your weight on your left leg. Shift your weight to your right leg (2) and bring your left leg forward. Lift your right knee (3) up high to the right side of your body. Shoot your kick out straight to the side (4) leading with the edge of your right foot. The lift and kick should be done in a single motion. At full extension (5) the muscle in your right leg and the entire right side of your lower back and buttocks should be completely tense. Notice the hand positions at this point. Release tension (6) and simply bring your right foot back with your eyes still on your target. Drop your right leg (7&8) and assume the original position.

Kick and Punch Combinations

Step Up—Front Kick—Double Punch

Start with your right foot back (1) and most of your weight on your right leg. Then (2) shift your weight to your left leg and (3) bring your right leg forward. Draw your left foot up and forward in an arching motion (4-6) so that your left knee seems to rush toward the left side of your chest. At full extension (7) the left side of your stomach, the calf muscles of your kicking leg and the upper back side of your supporting leg should all be completely tense; your body position should be leaning backwards slightly to give you more hip power. After you release tension (8) in one complete motion, lower your left leg (9) then turn your right shoulder and right fist to point at your opponent while your left hand draws back to get ready for the first punch. As soon as your left leg drops to the ground (10-14) punch forward with your left hand. Immediately after that (15-17) counter with your right hand.

Step Up—Roundhouse Kick—Double Punch

Begin (1) with your right foot forward. Without your opponent noticing (2), bring your left leg forward and shift your weight onto it. As you begin your kick (3&4) keep your hands in a comfortable position. Then at full extension (5) drop your right elbow back as your right hand whips across. The right side of your back should be tightly arched and your right leg should be tense. At this point, you should be looking over your shoulder at your target. Release tension (6) and bring your right leg back with your knees still up high. Then (7-9) begin dropping your right leg forward, and as soon as it touches the ground (10&11), reach out with your right shoulder and right fist to get ready for a counterpunch. At this point (12&13) counterpunch with your left hand.

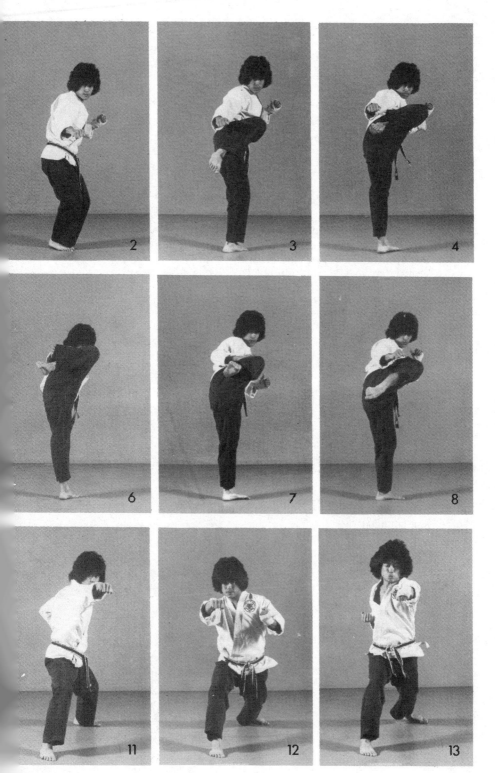

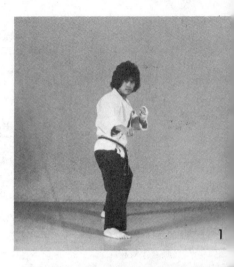

Step Up—Side Kick— Double Punch

Begin (1) with your right foot forward. Then bring your left leg forward (2) while looking directly at your opponent. Use your right hand to measure the distance between you and your opponent. Bring your right foot and knee up high (3) without your upper body leaning backwards. In order to do this, practice stretching exercises against a wall. Drop your right elbow back (4) as your right hand whips across. The backside of your thigh and your calf should be tightly extended. Release tension (5) and bring your right leg back with your knee still up high. Begin (6) dropping your right leg forward and as it touches the ground (7) reach out with your right shoulder and your right fist to get ready for a counterpunch. Immediately (8&9) counterpunch with your left hand.

2

3

5

6

8

9

Step Up—Side Kick—Back Kick—Punch

Begin with your right foot back (1) placing most of your weight on it. Shift your weight to your left leg only slightly (2) and bring your right leg forward. Then (3) lift your left knee up high to the left side of your body. Shoot your kick out straight to the side (4&5) leading with the edge of your left foot. The lift and kick should be done in a single motion, with the upper part of your body thrusting backwards. At full extension (6) the muscles in your left leg and the entire left side of your lower back and buttocks should be completely tense. Release tension (7) and simply withdraw your left leg. Then drop your left leg forward (8&9) and get ready for the next kick by turning your left heel (10) toward your opponent. Most of your weight should still be on your right leg. Turn your right shoulder and elbow (11) to your right while looking over your right shoulder. With most of your weight on your left leg (12) begin moving your right leg toward your opponent. Then (13) lift your right knee up high to the right side of your body. Shoot your kick out straight to the side (14) leading with the edge of your right foot. The lift and kick should be done in a single motion. At full extension (15) the muscles in your right leg and the entire right side of your lower back and buttocks should be completely tense. Release tension (16) and begin lowering your right leg forward. As it touches the ground (17&18) reach out with the right side of your body to get ready for the counterpunch. Immediately (19&20) counter with your left hand.

Double Punch—Roundhouse Kick—
Spin Back Crescent

Start (1) with your right foot forward. Then (2) punch with your right hand and immediately follow that by (3) countering with your left hand. As soon as you hear the snap of your punch (4) twist your upper body to the right, lifting your left knee up high. Swing your knee (5) and extend your foot forward in an arching motion. Retract (6&7) your leg and when it drops (8), land on the ball of your left foot. Then (9&10) look back to your right. While your body continues turning, and with your right elbow and right shoulder leading the move, (11&12) spin your right leg around. Use this momentum to kick your leg up high toward the right side of your chest while thrusting your right hip forward. Full extension (13) should begin just right of the imaginary center line, and it should continue as you move to the middle. At this point the calf and lower thigh of your kicking leg and the right side of your stomach should be completely tense. Then (14) use all the muscles in the back of your right leg and the top of your thigh to slam your right leg straight down, loosening them again (15) just as you settle into a right stance.

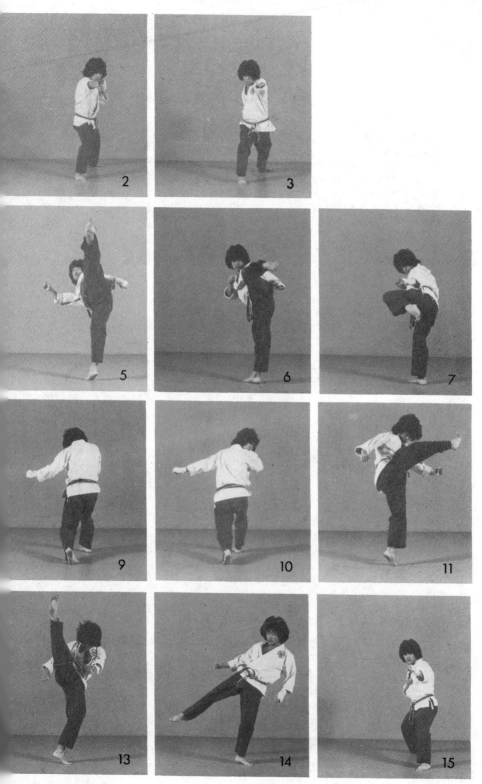

Double Punch—Roundhouse Kick—Spin Back Crescent—Step In—Side Kick—Punch

Start (1) with your right foot back. Punch (2) with your left hand and (3) immediately counterpunch with your right hand. Then (4) pick your right knee up high to get ready for a kick and (5) extend your foot forward as your body faces the left side. Drop your right elbow back (6) as your right hand whips across. The right side of your back should be tightly arched and your right leg should be completely tense. At this point you should be looking over your shoulder at your target. Release tension (7) and bring your right leg back with your knee still up high. Begin (8) dropping your right leg forward and (9) as it touches the ground, get ready for a spin. The heel of your right foot (10) should come off the ground and turn toward your target as you pivot. Shift your weight to the right foot (11-14) and continue turning; first your shoulders and hips and then your leg. As your left leg lifts and straightens, bend forward at your waist, drop-

Continued on next page

1

5

9

1C

Continued on next page

14

Continued from preceding page
ping your left hip down. At full extension (15) your kicking foot should be tense but your body should be loose and striving for maximum speed as the four moving parts blend together. For maximum power (16) your foot should be traveling on a line running horizontally with your target. Then (17) relax as your kick continues its circular course and (18) drop down with your left leg behind. As soon as your left leg touches the ground (19), start shifting your weight to your right leg and (20) move your left leg forward. Then (21) pick your right leg up to get ready for a side kick. At full extension (22) the muscles in your right leg and the entire right side of your lower back and buttocks should be completely tense. Release the tension (23) and start bringing your leg back. Simply drop your right leg (24) down and forward and (25) start reaching out with your right shoulder and fist to get ready for a counterpunch. Immediately (26) counterpunch with your left hand.

18

22

23

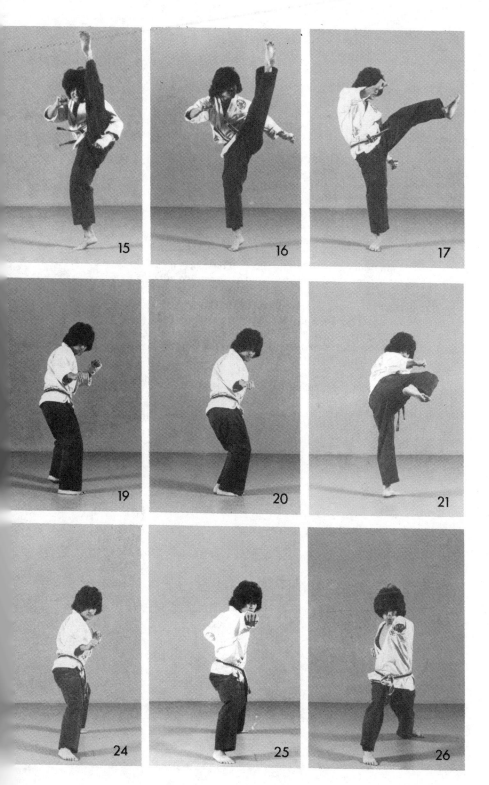

Jumping Crescent—Roundhouse Kick—Punch

Begin (1) with your right leg back. Shift your weight (2) to your left leg. Then (3) scoop your left foot and (4) jump off on your left foot. Thrust your left leg (5) to full extension while still in the air and (6) land on your right leg. The entire left leg and the left side of your body should be completely tightened. Notice in (7) how the left hand extends in front of the kick. After the foot passes center (8-10) draw it down and back in a slight arch, settling into a right stance. Next (11) twist your upper body to the left as if you're throwing a right punch. Then (12) lift your right knee to the side, and (13) as your leg extends, the muscles in your stomach and the entire right side of your back should be completely tightened. Retract your leg along the same path (14) moving your right foot back to return. Drop (15) your right leg calmly to the ground and (16) as soon as it touches the ground, reach out with your right hand to get ready for a counterpunch. Immediately (17) counterpunch with your left hand.

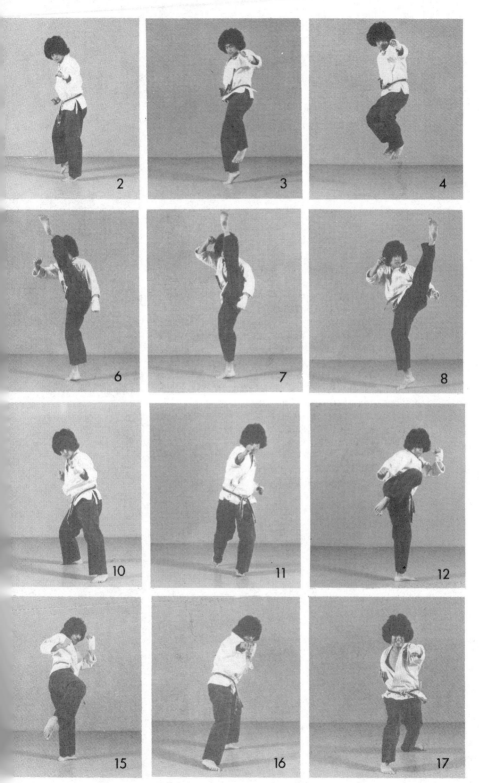

Step Up Hook Kick—Roundhouse Kick—Spinback Hook Kick—Punch

Begin (1) with your right foot back and most of your weight on your left leg. Then (2) bring your right leg forward to your left leg. Put all your weight on your right leg and (3) pick your left leg up and outward. Near full extension (4-6), jerk your left hip and shoulder to the left. Tighten the back of your left leg and the left side of your lower back to achieve the powerful whipping hook. Keep your left foot as tight as possible as it continues its motion (7) snapping it back to a cocked position. Lower your left foot (8&9) directly in front of you and (10) twist your upper body to the left as if throwing a right punch. Move your right hip forward (11) as you bring your right knee up in front of you, brushing your right foot closely

Continued on next page

2

3

5

6

7

9

10

11

Continued on next page

Continued from preceding page

past your left leg. At full extension (12) the muscles in your right leg should be tense and the right side of your back should be tightly arched. Release the energy (13&14) and retract your leg along the same path. As your right foot is dropped, (15) shift your weight back to your right leg and (16) turn to the left 180 degrees, pivoting so that the heel of your right foot comes off the ground and turns toward your target. As you shift your weight onto your right leg (17), snap your head around over your left shoulder in order to look at your opponent, and start moving your left foot toward your target. Next (18&19), lead with your left foot in a tight-hooking motion, arching your left knee up past your chest. At full extension (20) the left side of your lower back should be tightly arched and the back of your left leg should be pulling against the centrifugal force of your extending leg. Relax tension (21) and allow the momentum of your left foot to bend your left knee, then (22) drop your left foot to the floor in front of you. Immediately (23) counterpunch with your right hand.

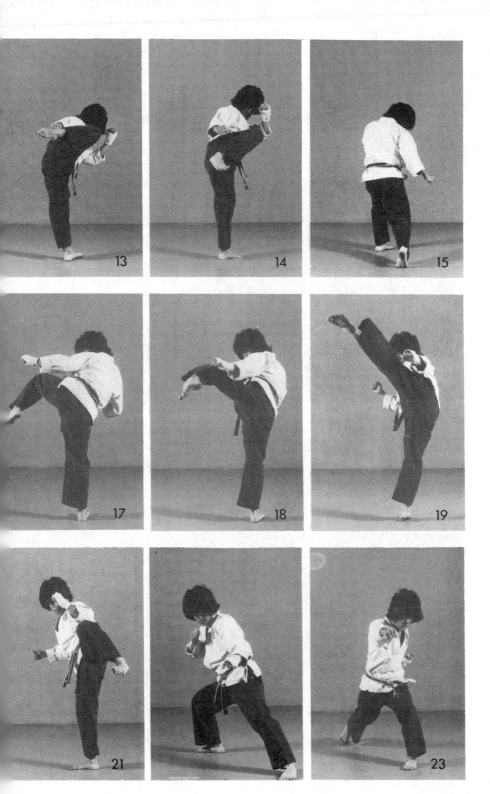

Punch—Drop Kick

Begin (1) with your right leg back. Then (2) as you shift your weight forward, reverse punch with your left hand. Begin pulling your punch back (3) with most of your weight on your front leg. Drop (4) and

bring both of your feet completely off the ground. At full extension (5), the muscles on your right leg should be tense and the right side of your back should be tightly arched.

Running Jumping Kicks

Running Jumping Front Kick

Begin (1) with a preferred stance. Then (2-4) run toward your target with your eyes focused directly at your opponent. Shift your weight to your forward leg (5-7), scoop your left foot in front of your right knee and jump off with your right leg so that it passes your left foot again. Your left foot should appear to be touching an invisible step. As you lead with your right hip (8) your right leg continues and thrusts, and the left leg is held in a cocked position. At full extension (9) your entire right leg and the right side of your lower back should be completely tightened. In competition, it is a good idea to extend the non-kicking foot toward the floor.

Running Jumping Roundhouse Kick

Begin (1) with a preferred stance. Then (2&3) start running toward your opponent. As your right leg comes forward (4&5) scoop your left foot in front of your right knee and jump off with your right leg so that it passes your left foot again. At this point (6) start turning your upper body to your left and lead your right hip outward. Your body (7) should now be completely turned to the left and your right foot should be cocked. At full extension (8), your entire right leg and the right side of your lower back should be completely tightened.

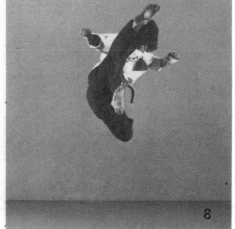

Running Jumping Side Kick

Begin (1) with a preferred stance. Then (2&3) start running at your opponent. With your right leg forward and off the ground (4) jump up with your left leg and lead with your right foot. As soon as your are off the ground (5) turn your body to the left with both legs cocked, leading with the edge of your right foot. Be sure to hold the edge of

your right foot parallel to the ground. At full extension (6) the muscles in your right leg and the entire right side of your lower back and buttocks should be completely tightened. Also notice the hand positions in (6). **Note:** A major concern with this kick is bringing your right foot up and out in a straight line without arching.

Running Jumping Back Kick

Begin (1) with a preferred stance. Then (2-4) start running at your opponent. With your right foot leading (5) slow down and, with most of your weight on your right leg (6) move your left leg as though you were taking another step. Jump off with your right leg (7&8) spinning clockwise while blocking with your left hand. As you turn keep your knees bent and your feet tucked up. At this point (9) your body should be moving forward from the running force. At full extension (10) your right foot should be tightened and the right side of your back should be tightly arched. Try your best to lock your hip in at full extension.

Running Jumping Spinning— Back Hook Kick

Begin (1) with a preferred stance. Then (2&3) start running at your opponent, taking as many steps as you wish. With your left leg forward (4) put all your weight on it and prepare to jump. Jump off the left leg (5) rising and spinning clockwise. Tuck your left leg up beneath you (6) and cock your right leg up high near the right side of your chest. Keeping it parallel to the ground. Extend your right leg up in a circular arch (7) while arching your back. Drop your right shoulder backwards to hook your kick across. Near full extension of your kick, your left leg should be reaching for the ground. However, do your best to keep your left leg up.

Running Jumping Crescent Kick

Begin (1) with a preferred stance. Then (2) start running at your opponent, taking as many steps as you wish. As your right foot reaches forward (3) put all your weight on it and prepare for a jump. Jump off your right leg (4) spinning clockwise. While in the air (5) snap your right shoulder, hip and leg around, straightening your kicking leg as it sweeps across in front of you. Your right foot and the outside of your kicking leg should be tightened as your leg shoots across. Your stomach should tighten to pull your weight forward into the kick. After the kicking extension (6) drop your left leg down to touch the floor. Then (7&8) let your body spin until your right foot falls behind your left foot.

Double Front Kick

Begin (1) with a preferred stance. Then (2-4) start running with your eyes focused on your target. Shift your weight to your right leg (5) and scoop your left foot in front of your right knee. Jump off with your right leg (6) as if both knees will touch your shoulders. Line up your legs parallel to each other (7) and begin to thrust them with the same power. At full extension (8) your legs and both sides of your lower back should be completely tightened.

Double Roundhouse Kick

Begin (1) with a preferred stance. Then (2&3) start running with your eyes focused on your target. Shift your weight to your right leg (4) and jump off with it. As soon as you are off the ground (5) turn your body to the left by turning your shoulder, waist and hip. Since your right leg is leading, it will be difficult for you to strike with both legs at the same time. However, (6) try to line up your legs parallel to each other so that they will be together at full extension. At this point (7) your upper body should be leaning almost parallel to the ground. Your right hand has whipped across to the right with both legs thrust into the target. However, you will find that the leading leg (in this case, the right leg) has slightly more power than the other.

Air Kick Combinations

Flying Side Kick
and Punch in the Air

Begin (1) with a preferred stance. Then (2) start running at your opponent. With your left leg forward (3) and with all your weight on it, jump off the ground. Immediately (4) turn your body to the left. Both legs should be cocked (5) and you should be leading with the edge of your right foot. Be sure to hold the edge of your right foot parallel to the ground. At this point (6) prepare for your punch. At full extension (7) the muscles in your right leg and the entire right side of your lower back and buttocks should be completely tense along with the punch.

Note: These movements should be done simultaneously; however, you may also kick before you deliver your punch.

2

4

5

7

SIDE VIEW

Double Front Kick in the Air

Begin (1) with a preferred stance. Then (2) start running at your opponent. As your right foot reaches forward (3&4), scoop your left foot in front of your right leg and begin cocking your right foot up. Kick out immediately with your left leg (5) with your upper body leaning slightly forward. Release tension on your left leg, and immediately kick with your right leg (6). At full extension, your entire right leg and the right side of your lower back should be completely tightened.

4

FRONT VIEW

Front Kick Round-house in the Air

Begin (1) with a preferred stance. With your right foot forward (2) scoop your left foot in front of your right knee and (3) jump off with your right leg. Begin cocking your right foot up. Immediately (4) kick out with your left leg, with your left shoulder preceding the kick. Bring your right knee up as high as possible (5) while re-

tracting your left leg. At this point, your upper body should be turning toward the left. When it has completely turned to the left and your right foot is cocked (6), complete the kick. At full extension, your entire right leg and the right side of your lower back should be completely tightened.

Front Kick—Side Kick in the Air

Begin (1) with a preferred stance. Then (2) start running at your opponent. With all your weight on your left leg, (3) scoop your right foot in front of your left leg. Jump off (4) with your left leg. Kick out immediately with your right leg (5) with your upper body leaning slightly forward. Bring your left knee up (6) as high as possible while retracting your right leg. At this time (7) you are getting ready to look to the left. When your left knee reaches its highest point, (8) begin bending your upper body slightly to the right. At the peak of the jump (9) shoot your leg out horizontally. At full extension (10) the left side of your lower back and your left buttocks should be completely tense.

7

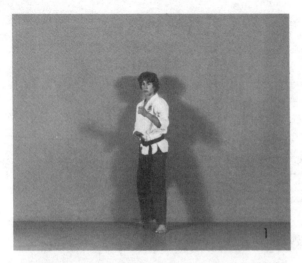

Scissor Kick

Begin (1) with a preferred stance. Then (2-4) start running at your opponent. Put all your weight on your left leg and begin the jump. Once you are completely in the air (5) lean your upper body slightly forward and to your left. Cock your right foot up high, parallel to the ground. The ball of your left foot should be facing

to the left. Simultaneously (6) lock your hip in when making the side kick with your right leg and the angular kick with your left leg. At full extension, the muscles in your right leg, the entire right side of your lower back and the calf muscles of your left leg should be completely tightened.

Scissor Kick and Punch

Begin (1) with a preferred stance. Then (2-4) start running at your opponent. Put all your weight on your left leg and begin the jump. Once you are completely in the air (5) lean your upper body slightly forward and to your left. Cock your right foot up high parallel to the ground. The ball of your left foot should be facing to the left. At this point, get ready to punch for-

ward. Simultaneously, (6) lock your hip in when making the side kick with your right leg and the angular kick with your left leg. At full extension, the muscles in your right leg, the entire right side of your lower back and the calf muscles of your left leg should be completely tense. Deliver the punch simultaneously with your kicks.

Split Front Kick

Begin (1) with a preferred stance. Then (2) start running at your opponent(s). When you are ready to kick (4) put your feet together and squat down. Reach both hands back as far as possible. When you jump (5) push off with both legs. As your arms and

shoulders turn to the center, thrust your kick out. At full extension, both legs and your lower back should be completely tightened.
Note: Pay close attention to the extension of the balls of the feet in (5).

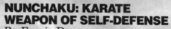